C000140402

Transcen

Essence of Self:

Essay on Peter Beagle's "The Last Unicorn"

By

Emalea Dickerson

Within Peter Beagle's "The Last Unicorn", there is a spiritual awakening taking place within the main character the unicorn, in human form the unicorn is also known as the Lady Amalthea in the novel. Her position in the novel questions the differences between the states of immortality associated with the soul, spirit, and essence of self. The progression of the storyline allows for the unicorn to traverse several layers of immortality which manifest themselves in the human, animal and immortal creatures. These states alter the unicorn's perceptions by holding to the magical Laws of Contagion that states, "Things that were one in contact continue to be connected after the connection is severed" (Frazier 138). This Law contain both the Law of Similarity, "Things that are alike are the same" (Frazier 138) and the Law of Sympathy "Magic that depends on the apparent association or agreement between things." (Frazier 138).

These specific definitions of magical law apply to the physical and spiritual presence of the unicorn to other living beings and the effect it has upon the unicorn's "'core'" self, transferring the innate concepts of both soul and spirit into her essence of self. These three states of being must be directly experienced in order for her to fully grasp the concepts of passion, time, and death, which are incomprehensible to her in the beginning of the story. The unicorn evolves from a dissociated immortal creature into a hero, which contains and exudes elements of all three states of being.

The first state of immortality which the unicorn is exposed to is that of the spirit which must have both an end of life and a rebirth into another living vessel. A spirit incorporates a beginning as a birth, a middle otherwise known as a lifespan, and the end which can be interpreted as a death. These three states of the spirit are in a continuously regenerating cycle that are determined by the presence of natural instinct and must be inherited on a genetic level that does not require conscience thought. The spirit also exists internally, cannot be seen with the naked eye, consists of personal power achieved by contact with other living things, and is applied to all living mortal creatures such as plants and animals (Frazier, summary, 119-212).

The concept of time is imperative to the regenerating cycle of the state of spirit, and its future impact on the Law of Contagion, when the unicorn encounters the butterfly "Psyche- the Greek term for butterfly is also 'soul'" (Cordry 34). The unicorn expresses concern at its presence, "You'll take cold and die before your time" (Beagle 12). This shows that despite the unicorns immortality she is aware of the passing of time and that death and a short life is common for some creatures, "They mean well, but they can't keep things straight. And why should they? They die so soon" (Beagle 13). With the butterfly's apparently short life, it could not have direct knowledge of the event leading to the disappearance of the unicorns people, it could not have direct experience with previous encounters of unicorns. The abundance of knowledge contained within the butterfly is a sign of the butterfly's spiritual value that can be compared to that of a shaman.

The butterfly serves dual roles in the novel "In contrast to the immortal unicorn, the butterfly seems to symbolize Time…Jumbling everything together regardless of quality…A butterfly is a creature of a day, transient, ephemeral…" (Norford 94). It is within the word transient, that the life of the butterfly is brought into focus. Transient can be interpreted as transitory a reference to the butterfly's brief mortal existence that can be applied to an altered state of consciousness such as prophecy. The butterfly is both time and prophecy to aspects found within the ideal of spirit. It displays this when is capable of communication with, and recognizing, the supernatural being as an immortal unicorn, and interprets transient from a shortened lifetime into an altered state of consciousness.

The confirmation of the butterfly's importance is affirmed as a shaman that is defined as "A religious specialist, who receives his or her power directly from the spirit world, acquires status, and the ability to do things through personal communication with the supernatural" (Stein 264). It is by affirming the butterfly its status that the spiritual element of its statements has a direct link with the spirit world. Despite a brief existence which would usually render the unicorn uninterested, she is focused on what the butterfly has to say once the creature recognizes her and is able to identify what she is, "Your name is a golden bell hung in my heart. I would break my body to pieces to call you once by your name…Unicorn. Old French, unicorne. Latin, unicornis. Literally, one-horned: unus, one, and cornu, a horn. A fabulous animal resembling a horse with one horn…" (Beagle 14). The butterfly's identification is important because it reaffirms the unicorns sense of existence, a shaman is recognized for its ability to correctly identify something which it has never before personally encountered. The butterfly is able to name the unicorn despite humankinds inability to identify what she is, "There were few men who gave chase but always to a wandering white mare; never in the gay and reverent manner proper to the pursuit of a unicorn… I could understand it if men had simply forgotten unicorns….But not to see them at all, to look at them and see something else- What do they look like to one another then…" (Beagle 12). This brings the butterfly's character into further clarity and creates a link between the two. The ongoing link, in addition to reconfirming the unicorn's sense of purpose, also provides information, on both the direction she should travel and the potential threat of the Red Bull.

The butterfly is using death as a metaphor for the Red Bull when it explains to the unicorn what has happened to her people. There is not a limitation on the explanation on the Bulls effect on just the unicorns, but it encompasses the Bulls impact on all beings, "You can find your people if you are brave. They passed down all the roads long ago, and the Red Bull ran close behind them and covered their footprints…His firstling bull has majesty, and his horns are the horns of a wild ox. With them he shall push the peoples, all of them, to the ends of the earth…" (Beagle 15). The butterfly emphasizes how death comes for all beings, including unicorns. Despite the unicorns being in possession of a commonly known form of immortality, death can still find her, and her people. The unicorn faces the incarnation of death in the form of the Red Bull upon her first contact with it "He was too strong, "she said "too strong. There was no end to his strength, and no beginning. He is older than I." (Beagle 147). The unicorn realizes that death comes for all beings; she has firsthand experience now in seeing death as real and with power over her. When their 'footprints are covered' they will essentially be removed from existence. This clarity reintegrates the value of those creatures that possess a soul and spirit, their continued existence is a part of their cycle of life and death. The unicorn's realization of this is essential to her continued journey through the aspects of immortality.

Immortal beings do not have an afterlife, once they 'die' they do not continue on in any form. This is why their essence of self is visible to the naked eye, they are in fact their power, and they do not contain a 'hidden' self-such as soul or spirit. This is a commentary on how the unicorns will not continue after death as those with an immortal spirit or soul will do, but instead will be wiped from the earth as if they had never existed. This is an example of the butterfly's role as a shaman as it relates to prophetic divination, in that the butterfly offers itself as such to the unicorn.

The butterfly is acting as a diviner that is an aspect of a shaman and is defined as "someone who practices divination, a series of activities that are used to obtain information about things that are not normally knowable. This may include things which will happen in the future, things that are occurring at the present time but at a distance, and things that touch the supernatural" (Fraizer 131-132). By utilizing its spiritual powers to assist the unicorn, giving its visions as both warning and challenge, the butterfly solidifies the ideal of spirit in the novel and its adherence to the Laws of Magic is reconfirmed.

The unicorn believes the Red Bull to be something that the butterfly had made up, she being unable to recognize the shamanic aspect of the butterfly. The concept of death having affected her kind is foreign and the unicorn is unable to process the information. The unicorn understands very little of actual emotion or imagination, and an immortals death is outside of her experiences. She continues with this correlation the butterfly makes by reciting a poem, "Sooner than I will live with you. / Fish will come walking out of the sea, /Sooner than you will come back to me." (Beagle 17). The unicorn does not know that the butterfly's presence has already affected her by giving her a prophetic sense in the form of poetry. The unicorn will discover later in the novel that her people were trapped in the sea by the Red Bull, "But they would not come to land while the Bull was there. They rolled in the shallows swirling together … no longer with the sea, but losing it. Hundreds were borne in with each swell and hurled against the ones already struggling to keep from being shoved ashore, and they in their turn struck out desperately, rearing and stumbling… " (Beagle 267). The poem is an echo of the unicorns people trapped in the sea; it is a hint which came to the unicorn of what she is capable of, that she will not be a victim, but instead rise up.

The narrative explains how the unicorn, "did not understand the words…but she had heard autumn beginning to shake the beech trees the very moment that she stepped out into the road." (Beagle 17) Autumn is used as a transitional phase which preludes winter; there are implications of death and rebirth, the essential spirit, in the changes of the seasons, as change has already found the unicorn, reshaping and strengthening her as passively and lightly as the wings of a butterfly.

The second state of immortality encountered by the unicorn is the soul. The word soul is used to define "...the non-corporeal, spiritual component of an individual...l" is limited to "...the spirits which inhabit a human body..." and "...usually has an existence after death..." (Stein 161). The soul must consist of the belief of an afterlife as is applicable in the novel to the fundamental Christian concepts of Heaven, Hell, Purgatory, and/or the continuation of a being after death. The soul must have the presence of the internal conscience that is limited to those characters which are in possession of a soul, thus limited to mortal human beings. Finally the soul must be hidden by external perception which means it cannot be seen by the naked eye, the soul is hidden within the human body.

It is with the first in-depth conversation the unicorn holds with a human being that the lack of conscience within the immortal begins to define the unicorn's perception of humanity, "I can never regret." (Beagle 58), this statement by the unicorn is profound, for human beings regret and the unicorn does not. It requires conscience thought to regret choices, to not do so, ever, confirms that the unicorn is comprised of a being whose thoughts and actions are one. As a result, the unicorn's perceptions of the world is almost an incomprehensible philosophical lens. This "'lens'" is one which is without the basic building blocks of humanity, which in the novel includes a belief system based upon Christian ideology. Right and wrong are not a part of the unicorns thought process, she is not driven by emotion. What she feels comes to her over the course of ages, not the flash of emotions found in mortal man. It is because of this that the unicorn's eyes reflect not the mortality of man, but her own immortality. The unicorn's eyes hold what is most dear to herself, "What is the matter with your eyes? They are full of green leaves, crowded with trees and streams and small animals. Where am I? Why can I not see myself in your eyes?" (Beagle 170). Humanity and the natural life span of a human which accumulates in a passage of the soul into a different existence is a pale reflection of the depth found in the immortal.

The unicorn hides nothing, she contains no hidden self or secret thoughts, what she is, is always upon her, no matter what form she wears. It is not a lack of caring but a lack of desire or possession in the unicorn which alienates her from human beings, "Unicorns know nought of need, or shame, or doubt, or debt- but mortals, as you may have noticed, take what they can get" (Beagle 48). It is by the lack of understanding of need that the unicorn learns that love is a form of possession for some beings and of sacrifice for others.

The unicorn's people are hunted and captured by the Red Bull, who is merely a servant of King Haggard who desired to possess all of the unicorns and hired a wizard to produce the Red Bull to serve him. To the king the possession of the unicorns and the love of the unicorns is the same thing. In the unicorn's existence, she had never loved in regards to a spiritual attachment to another being, and/or a physical 'love'. This emphasizes the unicorn's purity as a virgin, and further disconnects her from the cycle of the spirit. It also shows a correlation between the human concepts of possession and love. Love is an aspect of the soul, but so is possession as a human must be in possession of a soul in order to love. The unicorn was, "Alone in her lilac wood, indifferent to time and the round of birth and death" (Norford 94). The unicorn had never loved another, this did not mean that she herself was not loved by others. It was her own separation of her being from the world around her as a detached observer which immured her to the passage of time. Her detachment is what stifled her understanding of love and human passions.

The unicorn is positioned in the novel to examine her understanding of the value of man's mortality; of the driving passions of their feelings, such as her relationship with Prince Lir the adopted son of King Haggard. Prince Lir is in love with the Lady Amalthea, "And all for nothing," he said. "I cannot touch her, whatever I do. For her sake, I have become a hero- I, sleepy Lir, my father's sport and shame- but I might just as well have remained the dull fool I was. My great deeds mean nothing to her." (Beagle 178). The Lady Amalthea does not value Prince Lir, or his deeds.

The Lady Amalthea was more concerned with Prince Lir's horse whom she could not heal than any display from the prince, "She wept when my horse's legs did not heal-I heard her weeping- and yet there were no tears in her eyes when she ran away. Everything else was there, but no tears." (Beagle 181). It is from the sustainable contact with Schmendrick, Molly and Prince Lir that enables the unicorn to grasp the basic principles of a soul as the Lady Amalthea. The unicorn begins to value her companion's for their ability to perceive that which she cannot. And with her own personal experiences as the Lady Amalthea, she relies upon them to guide her, much like a child to parents. For ultimately man's existence hinges upon its mortality yet still contains an immortal soul, and thus, the capacity to love.

It is Schmendrick and Molly who show the unicorn the diversity of human's love and because of her magical nature she is influenced by them, absorbing aspects of them both. When the unicorn first encounters Schmendrick the Magician she is very dismissive of him until she realizes he also is immortal thus more real to her than the mortals. The immense age of the unicorn prohibits any real attachment to mortal creatures they are almost a dream to her as memories fade over time. Schmendrick has a concept of time which the unicorn observes, "For I too am real. I am Schmendrick the Magician, the last of the red-hot swamis, and I am older than I look." (Beagle 44). The unicorn and Schmendrick are linked because of similar sympathetic magic which affects their states of immortality, unlike the unicorn Schmendrick immortality is a curse placed upon him by his mentor the wizard Nikos.

As Schmendrick states upon his first encounter is that he is also real, and that reality, which includes a cycle of death, is what the unicorn questions most about humanities existence. The spell which Schmendrick casts upon the unicorn to save her life from being extinguished by the Red Bull is an echo of his mentor. It is a similar form of sympathetic magic that is used on the unicorn by Schmendrick,

…Her trapped terror was more lovely than any joy…, and that was the most terrible thing about it … the girl crouched on the ground and spoke…"What have you done to me?" …"I will die here" She tore at the smooth body and blood flowed her fingers. "I will die here! I will die!" Yet there was no fear in her face…Her face remained quiet and untroubled… "I am myself still. This body is dying. I can feel it rotting all around me. How can anything that is going to die be real? How can it be truly beautiful?" (Beagle 146-150)

The Unicorn does not fear death as the Lady Amalthea, because she still thinks of herself as purely unicorn, untainted by humanity's mortality. The unicorn does not comprehend the human soul, the progression of the spell on the Lady brings later comprehension but it is the spell itself which defines the role of Schmendrick to the unicorn. Schmendrick casts the spell without intent, or will, in effect calling upon a greater power, in which he is its vessel. As a once mortal man Schmendrick does not exude the same power as other immortals such as the unicorn. His power is internal and hidden and his soul is the conduit to power. When Schmendrick appeals to a higher power or deity he is preforming as a priest, "A full time religious specialist who is associated with formalized religious institutions" (Stein 126-133). Schmendrick must be granted power from another source despite his immortality, whereas the unicorn is her power and can be view as her own source. This is why the power leaving Schmendrick and returning is such a personal, draining experience, souls are not meant to be sent out of the human body, and immortals are not meant to contain their essences. As the Lady Amalthea the unicorn must contain her essence, Schmendrick never really grasps the underline meaning of containing that much of the unicorns self, yet Molly does.

When the unicorn encounters Molly she is compelled to say something to her, the unicorn does not yet grasp the meaning behind the first encounter with Molly, "Where have you been?" Before the whiteness and the shining horn, Molly shrank to a shining beetle…it was the unicorn's old dark eyes that looked down. "I am here now…" (Beagle 97). The unicorn's puzzlement at Molly is apparent, she allows Molly to join her, yet it is unknown what force drives her to do so. The unicorn accepts Molly's presence and her forgiveness, despite the reasoning that this unicorn had done nothing directly to her. In this encounter the unicorn realizes that she has indeed "'done nothing'" in her immortal existence, the unicorn realizes that she had never before been positioned to live up to the mortals perception of the "'ideal'" unicorn. It is by this realization that the unicorn accepts Molly, unhindered. Schmendrick continues the conversation between Molly and the unicorn with "unicorns are not to be forgiven…Unicorns are for beginnings… for innocence and purity, for newness. Unicorns are for young girls." (Beagle 98). Schmendrick implies that Molly's presence and manner which she used to address the unicorn is disrespectful, he tries to persuade Molly not to join the unicorns quest, treating her as a piranha and unworthy of joining their quest. Molly who falls into the biblical role of Jezebel in the novel is in effect saved by the unicorns cleansing presence. Schmendrick is behaving as the outraged priest, whom has found his idol sullied by something foul and impure.

The unicorn is in essence the sacred presence which "binds people together" (Stein 15) and the sacred reality "that is beyond ordinary experiences" (Stein 15).

During the unicorns travels her group come across a prosperous town. While the encounter with the town was brief, the contact with the townsfolk shows the value and perception of human's ideological view point. By examining this viewpoint the unicorn can see how they view suffering, their immortal souls, and the value of self-examination, "We do lead a good life here, or if we don't, I don't know anything about it. I sometimes think that a little fear, a little hunger, might be good for us — sharpen our souls, so to speak…That's why we always welcome strangers…They broaden our outlook…set us to looking inward…" (Beagle 65). The unicorn uses Schmendrick the "'faith'" he inspires and his ability to act as priest to guide her in her mortal form; it is from this sympathetic magic that the unicorn is able to retain some aspects of the soul after her time as the Lady Amalthea. It gives the unicorn a larger viewpoint of the many aspects of love which includes virginity and purity, but can also include hardship and suffering.

The virginity of the unicorn is important to the concept of spirit and soul because, the unicorn is female, "A female unicorn. Beagle's unicorn has one quality that sets her apart from all her mythological and literary ancestors: She is female" (Cordry 22). The first lines of the novel are, "…and she lived all alone" (Beagle 1, and Cordy 22). This means that despite the fact that she was female she had never mated "They mate very rarely" (Beagle 2) and had never contributed to the continuation of life an essential part of the concept of a spirit. The unicorn is removed from the cycle, "Beagle's female unicorn thus combines the

unicorn and the virgin into one symbol"
(Cordy 23). Her detachment is essential in
understanding the dissociation the unicorn
has to other living creatures, "Generation
after generation, wolves and rabbits alike,
they hunted and loved and had children and
died, and as the unicorn did none of these
things, she never grew tired of watching
them." (Beagle 2). She in fact; is merely an
observer in the continuously regenerative
cycle of life and death.

The complete lack of the unicorn's
sexual identity only exists while it is a
unicorn, as the Lady Amalthea she identifies
at a more 'human' level. The unicorn
embodies virginity and the positive
associations with the word. Molly represents
procreation, with an implication of previous
sexual activity in their first encounter and

the regret which can accompany it from a human value system. All are part of a reoccurring cycle found in nature that the unicorn had previously observed in a detached almost clinical way, with the addition of human belief structures and a Christian biased ideology which encompasses mortal sins, a new understanding of relationships is presented to the unicorn. The unicorn welcomes Molly into her troupe because she is curious about her and wishes to continue to observe her. Molly frequently questions the Lady Amalthea's behavior, she acts as a handmaiden to the Lady, correcting her behavior and frequently offering advice and assistance. The unicorn as the Lady Amalthea is as an infant in her perceptions of human behavior, ""Cruel?" she asked. "How can I be cruel? That is for mortals." But then she did raise her eyes, and they were great with sorrow, and with something very near to mockery. She said, "So is kindness."…" (Beagle 185). The Lady understands the changes growing in her in mortal form, "The magician gave me only the semblance of a human being…the seeming, but not the spirit…" and confides in Molly, "Now I am two- myself, and this other that you call 'my lady' For she is here as truly as I am now, though once she was only a veil over me." (Beagle 186). It is from the sustainable contact with her companions, and the other human beings that the unicorn begins to succumb to the luxury of forgetting. The unicorn forgets exactly what she is and embraces the possibilities before her, which includes the possibility of loving Prince Lir. The Lady Amalthea understands that she is developing an immortal soul. The cost of a soul for the Lady Amalthea is the unicorn's possession of her essence of self, which embodies and empowers the immortality of the unicorn. Remaining as the Lady Amalthea would require her to forget about what makes the unicorn's immortality unique among the layers of immortality.

The essence of self is what separates a unicorn from an animal's spirit or a human's soul. Essence of self requires an immortal being who does not have instinct or conscience, which consists of both total lack of growth and development and the immortal does not consist of a hidden self The unicorn transverses through the experiences of others perceptions of their "selves" in order to become a hero who contains and exudes elements of all three. It is the Law of Similarity which makes this possible, from the first contact with the butterfly, to the interactions with the humans in her company, all of the events in the unicorns story leads to the final battle with the Red Bull, in which Prince Lir was killed protecting her, while she ran from death, The unicorn flashed by them-…and Prince Lir leaped into the path of the Red Bull…he fell without a cry…but then the unicorn turned. The Red Bull halted when she did, and wheeled to put her once more between himself and the sea…She stood motionless, staring at the twisting body of Prince Lir…"Suddenly the unicorn screamed. It was not at all like the challenging bell with which she had first met the Red Bull; it was an ugly, squawking wail of sorrow and loss and rage, such as no immortal creature ever gave." (Beagle 264-5).

In this moment the unicorn grasps that she holds within her a spirit and a soul, her experiences changed her, by forcing her essence of self to expand and engulf these two additional forms of immortality. She becomes more that what her people are, "The unicorns horn was light again, burning and shivering like a butterfly. (Beagle 265). Her horn is a manifestation of the spirit of the butterfly, the unicorn's shamanic guide. Her emotions once always projected outward now contain some hidden element, "She lunged after him, driving to kill, but she could not reach him. She might have been stabbing at a shadow, or a memory."(Beagle 266). The unicorn understands that she has changed, she is no longer a being which projects her inner being onto others, she remembers, sharply, clearly, and painfully. She rages against not just the Bull, but the driving passions within her, and what those drives means to her existence. For a moment in time the unicorn let's go of herself, her essence, and fully embraces the lessons imposed upon her by spirit and soul, and wins.

The unicorn does not fear death, "The unicorn lowered her head one last time and hurled herself at the Red Bull…the blow would have burst him like rotten fruit."(Beagle 267) she embraces it. She is driven to kill the creature which caused her such harm, to experience such profound loss. It is not a unicorn's instinct to kill, it is not an aspect of spirit to strike out for revenge or passion, and this is ultimately good or bad, a mortal expression of the soul. It was long that the unicorn stood by Prince Lir before she touched him with her horn. For all her quest had ended…there was weariness in the way she held herself, and a sadness in her beauty… It suddenly seemed to her that the unicorns sorrow was not for

Lir but for the lost girl who could not be brought back; for the Lady Amalthea, who might have lived happily ever after with the prince." (Beagle 271)

The unicorn resurrects the Prince, her newfound understanding of death, of passion, of the value of life, allows her to do so. Now; death, in all of its forms, no longer touches her, she lives with spirit, soul and essence combined. She cannot flee from her new self or change this. "My people are in the world again. No sorrow will live in my heart as long as that joy — save one, and I thank you for that, too. Farewell, good magician. I will try to go home."(Beagle 271) she understands that she can no longer be what she was before, she can never truly 'go home'.

By fully realizing the gift which was the Princes love, the unicorn knows what it means for death to come for him, his soul will live on untouchable, unchangeable, and without her. So the unicorn does the only thing she can, she says to him, offered like a gift, "I remember you. I remember." And flees. It is the Laws of Magic themselves which allow the unicorn to establish a new existence of immortality. Her priest, shaman, and self all contribute to her finality of a heroic being. She is no longer an animal with a spirit, a human with a soul, or a unicorn with an essences, but a new creature consisting of all three. It is by obtaining this higher level of immortality that the unicorn is in fact doomed, to be alone, and to remember. She holds within her a truly immortal spirit and soul, and will carry her sorrow, a part of her essence for all time, for death will never touch her now, she will

never cease to be.

———————————————

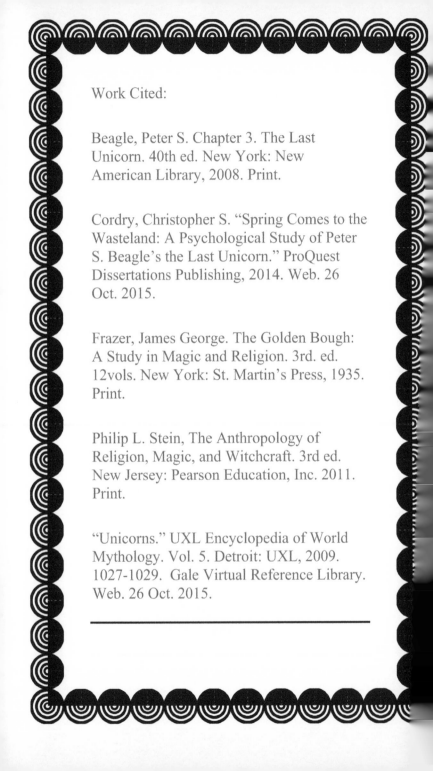

Work Cited:

Beagle, Peter S. Chapter 3. The Last
Unicorn. 40th ed. New York: New
American Library, 2008. Print.

Cordry, Christopher S. "Spring Comes to the
Wasteland: A Psychological Study of Peter
S. Beagle's the Last Unicorn." ProQuest
Dissertations Publishing, 2014. Web. 26
Oct. 2015.

Frazer, James George. The Golden Bough:
A Study in Magic and Religion. 3rd. ed.
12vols. New York: St. Martin's Press, 1935.
Print.

Philip L. Stein, The Anthropology of
Religion, Magic, and Witchcraft. 3rd ed.
New Jersey: Pearson Education, Inc. 2011.
Print.

"Unicorns." UXL Encyclopedia of World
Mythology. Vol. 5. Detroit: UXL, 2009.
1027-1029. Gale Virtual Reference Library.
Web. 26 Oct. 2015.

Norford, Don Parry. "Reality and Illusion in Peter Beagle's the Last Unicorn." Critique: Studies in Modern Fiction 19.2 (1977): 93. JSTOR. Web. 26 Oct. 2015.

Reiter, Geoffrey. "'Two Sides of the Same Magic': The Dialectic of Mortality and Immortality in Peter S. Beagle's the Last Unicorn."

Mythlore 27.105/106 (2009): 103-116. JSTOR. Web. 06 Oct. 2015.

Lightning Source UK Ltd.
Milton Keynes UK
UKHW040656220420
362071UK00001B/14

9 781705 389676